BRITISH AND COMMONWEALTH WAR CEMETERIES

Julie Summers

SHIRE PUBLICATIONS

Published in Great Britain in 2012 by Shire Publications
Ltd, Midland House, West Way, Botley, Oxford OX2 0PH,
United Kingdom.

44-02 23rd St, Suite 219, Long Island City, NY 11101

E-mail: shire@shirebooks.co.uk   www.shirebooks.co.uk

© 2010 Julie Summers. First printed 2010. Reprinted
2012.

Every attempt has been made by the Publishers to secure
the appropriate permissions for materials reproduced in
this book. If there has been any oversight we will be happy
to rectify the situation and a written submission should be
made to the Publishers.

A CIP catalogue record for this book is available from the
British Library.

Shire Library no. 596   •   ISBN-13: 978 0 74780 789 6

Julie Summers has asserted her right under the Copyright,
Designs and Patents Act, 1988, to be identified as the
author of this book.

Designed by Tony Truscott Designs, Sussex, UK
and typeset in Perpetua and Gill Sans.
Printed in China through Worldprint Ltd.

12 13 14 15 16   11 10 9 8 7 6 5 4 3 2

COVER IMAGE
Artillery Wood Cemetery, Ypres, Belgium.

TITLE PAGE IMAGE
Thiepval Memorial by Sir Edwin Lutyens, unveiled in
1932 to commemorate the 72,000 Missing of the Somme.

CONTENTS PAGE IMAGE
Caterpillar Valley Cemetery at Longueval on the Somme.

ACKNOWLEDGEMENTS
Julie Summers would like to extend warm thanks to the
following for their help and support: Andrew Baylay, Peter
Boyden, Judith Donald, Peter Francis, Nigel Haines, Roy
Hemmington, Roger Hess, Stephanie Hess, Nick Hewitt,
Emma Lefley, Rosie Llewellyn-Jones, Chris Lofty, Stephen
Rockcliffe, Steve Rogers, Rob Rowntree, and to Richard
Steele, her assiduous picture researcher, who found the
map of Cathcart's Hill Cemetery hidden in a file at the
Commonwealth War Graves Commission in Maidenhead,
amongst other treasures.

I should like to thank the following people and
organisations who have kindly allowed me to use
illustrations:
Peter Ashton, title page image; The Bermuda National
Trust, page 7; CWGC pages 8 (top), 9 (bottom), 10, 12,
14, 15, 16, 18, 22, 23, 24, 26 (top), 27 (top), 28 (top), 30
(bottom), 31 (bottom), 33 (top), 34, 40 (top), 41, 44
(top), 47 (top), 48 (bottom), 49 (top), 51, 56 (top), 58,
59; Luis Ferreira 50; Brian Harris, pages 3, 6 (middle and
bottom), 19, 28 (bottom), 31 (top), 32, 33 (bottom), 35,
36, 38, 40 (bottom), 42, 43, 44 (bottom), 45, 46, 47
(bottom), 48 (top), 49 (bottom), 56 (bottom), 57
(bottom), 60, 61, 63; Roger Hess, pages 11, 57 (top);
courtesy of the Council of the National Army Museum,
London, page 9 (top); Liam O'Connor, page 52 (bottom);
Jane McKinnon-Johnson, page 8 (bottom left); Noah R.
Martin Jr, page 8 (bottom); Ian Rank-Broadley, page 53;
Guido M Rincón, page 8 (bottom right). All other
photographs were taken by the author.

EDITOR'S NOTE
The correct modern spelling of Ypres is 'Ieper'. However,
most readers will be more familiar with the older spelling,
which we have therefore used throughout.

Shire Publications is supporting the Woodland Trust, the UK's leading woodland conservation charity, by funding the dedication of trees.

CONTENTS

INTRODUCTION

O N A SMALL BLUFF in the middle of the Umbrian countryside, with a stunning view of the great Duomo that dominates the skyline of the ancient hill town of Orvieto, lies a small war cemetery. It is entered through a gate in a yellow stone wall topped with white coping. A tiny open-sided tempietto with square fluted columns and a triangular pediment offers shelter from the sun and rain. A bronze door holds a register of the burials. At the back of the cemetery is a cross adorned with a bronze sword and there are 190 graves arranged in neat rows, evenly spaced and each engraved with the name, rank, age and date of death of a Commonwealth serviceman. These men, 183 Britons, three South Africans, and three Canadians, all died, with one exception, between 14 June and 4 July 1944.

The land on which the cemetery is constructed was a gift from the Italian people in perpetuity so that those men who fought in the Italian campaign north of Rome in 1944 might have a permanent resting place near the battlefield where they fell. Orvieto War Cemetery is one of some 23,000 burial locations in 150 countries dating from the First and Second World Wars cared for by the Commonwealth War Graves Commission.

More familiar, perhaps, are the First World War cemeteries that are strewn across the countryside of France and Belgium marking the sites of great battles in that 'war to end all wars': Mons, Loos, the Somme, Passchendaele. But why are they there? And what about the dead from earlier wars – from Waterloo, the Crimea and the South African Wars, to name but a very few?

The definition of a war cemetery has not formally been laid down but it is widely accepted that it represents a burial ground for service personnel who died during a war, as opposed to a cantonment or garrison cemetery, which might also contain the remains of the families of servicemen and of those who died of disease, accident or natural causes as a result of their service in places such as India, North America, the Caribbean or south-east Asia. This book deals only with the question of burial in a war cemetery.

Opposite: Orvieto War Cemetery, Umbria, contains the remains of 190 Commonwealth servicemen from three weeks of fighting in June and July 1944.

5

Right: The inscription at Orvieto reads:
'The land on which this cemetery stands
is the gift of the Italian people for the
perpetual resting place of the sailors,
soldiers and airmen who are honoured
here.'

Below: St Symphorien Military Cemetery
at Mons in Belgium was started by the
Germans in 1914. It has the distinction
of holding some of the first and last
casualties of the First World War. It was
laid out with great care by the Germans,
who held it until 1918.

Left: Etaples
Military Cemetery
contains the
graves of 10,771
Commonwealth
servicemen from
the First World
War. Relatively
few (thirty-five)
are unidentified
because the
majority of burials
came from the
fifteen hospitals
around the Etaples
area. There are a
further 119 from
the Second World
War and 662 non-
Commonwealth
burials, mainly
German.

Respect for fallen servicemen is a relatively new phenomenon and, shocking though it might now seem, public opinion of the Army in the pre-Crimean era was low. Wellington described his men with contempt: 'Our Army is composed of the scum of the earth – the mere scum of the earth.' Ordinary soldiers were buried in mass graves and usually only officers were accorded dignity in death and might be commemorated by a headstone or memorial if the regiment or family was prepared to fund it. A small number of senior officers were embalmed, or pickled in brandy, and brought back to the United Kingdom for burial at home. This casual treatment of the dead had to do with expediency and hygiene rather than disrespect; disease was an ever present threat to the armed forces, and up to the First World War more men died of disease than were killed in battles.

For hundreds of years the Navy has had its own tradition for sailors. In the unforgiving environment of the high seas the disposal of its dead differs from that of men who die on land, the most obvious being burial at sea. As Mark Quinlan, author of *Remembrance*, explains: 'The dead sailor [was] sewn into his hammock with the last stitch sewn through the nose (to ensure the corpse was indeed dead), followed by committal to the Deep under a white ensign.' Quinlan notes that this convention did not apply for all senior naval officers, some of whom were brought home for burial. There was also, in the Navy, the long-standing practice of reading the Service for the Dead even when no body was recovered.

The land on which the Royal Naval Cemetery on Ireland Island in Bermuda stands was purchased by the Royal Navy in 1809 and consecrated in 1812. The cemetery, also known as 'The Glade', was open to all for burial until 1849, when convicts were excluded. Many Royal Navy personnel are buried or commemorated, as are those who died of the yellow fever that ravaged the British military in Bermuda during the nineteenth century.

A memorial service off Helles in Gallipoli in the 1920s to commemorate those men who have no known grave but the sea.

Some garrison or cantonment cemeteries have become associated with battles of the eighteenth or nineteenth centuries, and this has led people to assume they are war cemeteries when they are not. One is Trafalgar Cemetery on Gibraltar. It was originally called Southport Ditch Cemetery and was consecrated in June 1798, seven years before the Battle of Trafalgar. Despite the obvious association, there are only two battle casualties buried in the cemetery, which fell into disuse in 1814. The remaining headstones paint a vivid picture of the history of the Rock and of the vital role of the naval operations in the area during the Napoleonic Wars. All this has been discovered only since the 1980s, when the cemetery underwent restoration.

During the Crimean War the seeds of change were sown. The use of the telegraph meant that commanders in London could issue instructions to the

Below left: William Forster is one of the two men who died in the Battle of Trafalgar and was buried in Trafalgar Cemetery.

Below right: Trafalgar Cemetery on Gibraltar was used by the British between 1798 and 1814 predominantly for military burials.

Army, thus reducing both its independence and its remoteness from Britain. The public had, for the first time, access to photographs and reports from the battlefield, mainly through copy sent back to *The Times* by the Irish reporter William Howard Russell, who spared no reputations. The reaction was one of horror and outrage. The immediate upshot was the provision of better

The Cemetery at Scutari, 1856: watercolour signed and dated by William Simpson. Two men are praying on the left in the foreground and a funeral procession is seen on the right with a hospital in the distance.

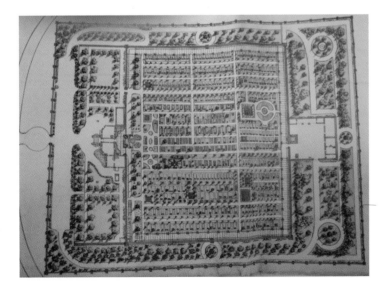

The CWGC took on responsibility for restoring the Crimean War cemetery at Cathcart's Hill. This drawing, dating from 1931, shows the layout of the cemetery, which was subsequently destroyed during the Second World War.

9

Haidar Pasha Cemetery contains burials from the Crimean, First and Second World wars, as well as graves from non-war military deaths and those of civilians.

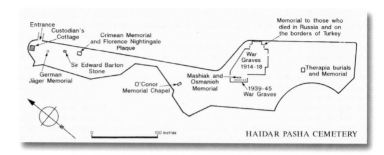

HAIDAR PASHA CEMETERY

The First World War plot in Haidar Pasha Cemetery contains the remains of 407 servicemen, of whom sixty are unidentified. There are a further thirty of the Second World War, fourteen being unidentified. There are five non-Commonwealth burials and seventy-six service burials not from the two world wars.

care for the sick and wounded but men still died of disease in huge numbers in comparison to those who died in the fighting. Some 2,750 men were killed in action and two thousand died of wounds, but more than sixteen thousand died of disease. Men who were killed during the battles were buried by their regiments in small cemeteries which have long since disappeared. Two cemeteries, at Haidar Pasha and Cathcart's Hill, survived and were restored during the 1920s but the latter was reduced to rubble during the Second World War. Haidar Pasha, however, still exists. Six thousand men, mostly victims of the 1853 cholera epidemic, were interred in a mass grave during the Crimean War. During the First World War the Turks used the cemetery to inter British prisoners of war who had died in captivity.

One of the issues that made commemoration of the dead of the Crimean War so difficult was the fact that no death certificates were issued,

and record keeping and casualty handling were haphazard. However, in 1988 a genealogist called Brian Oldham began an enormous project to amalgamate all the remaining records to compile the great Crimean War index.

A further change occurred at the end of the nineteenth century in the South African wars, when, for the first time, volunteers joined the armed forces to fight. The Army Medical Corps was alarmed to discover that 40 per cent of the men called up for duty were physically unfit to fight and, as with the Crimean War, the largest number of deaths occurred as a result of disease rather than the fighting. In all just over 280,000 men, including nearly fifty thousand volunteers, were recruited between 1899 and 1902 and of those six thousand were killed in action and a further two thousand died of wounds, but over thirteen thousand died of disease.

Now it was no longer acceptable to bury soldiers in a mass grave. Their families and the public demanded more respect be shown to the dead. In the past mass burial had been expedient and the removal of all personal effects, including teeth, was accepted – it would not have been uncommon for someone wearing false teeth in the nineteenth century to have a mouthful of teeth from a dead soldier – but this was no longer tolerated. During the Second Boer War (1899–1902) there was a step change: the Royal Engineers were tasked with recording the location of all British military graves of the war. A group called the Guild of Loyal Women was formed to locate graves, compile registers and mark the sites with iron crosses. In 1910 this was put on a more formal footing with the formation of the South African Soldiers' Graves Association, which took over responsibility for the work from the Guild. In all there were some 25,000 burials in 356 cemeteries. It was an enormous task to care for so many sites and without proper funding they soon fell into disrepair.

Above: This stone commemorates men who died in May and June 1900 and who were buried in Fort Knokke Cemetery but transferred to Maitland Cemetery in Cape Town in November 1927.

Left: A First World War headstone dedicated to the memory of Private Ashley Stennett, aged 22 years and 5 months. He died on Christmas Day 1916.

A GREAT CHANGE
FOR THE GREAT WAR

In 1914 everything changed. The First World War, the 'war to end all wars', resulted in deaths on a hitherto unimagined scale. The result was the biggest outpouring of public grief ever witnessed, prompting a major public arts programme in Britain and the founding of one of the most remarkable organisations of the twentieth century, the Imperial War Graves Commission. Several things happened simultaneously. Firstly, the growing awareness among the public since the South African wars that something had to be done about the disposal of the Army's dead was compounded with disquiet over the dilapidated state of the war cemeteries in the Transvaal. Secondly, the First World War was fought on land not thousands of miles away on a different continent but at its closest just tens of miles from home in France and Belgium. People felt much closer to the battles than they had done in the past. Thirdly, and probably most significantly, this was the largest volunteer army led into battle in British military history.

From today's perspective it is difficult to understand the intense patriotism felt by both sides of the conflict, with men eager to fight for their country. For the first eighteen months of the war on average 100,000 volunteers a month came forward, with almost the same number mobilised after conscription was introduced in Britain in 1916. In total the British Commonwealth and Empire mobilised nearly nine million men.

Although trench warfare was not new, it had never before been fought on such a scale nor over such a long period of time, nor, of course, with modern weapons, which continued to develop with astonishing rapidity and brutality throughout the war. Men wearing steel helmets were pitted against shells and mortars, grenades, machine guns, flame throwers, poison gas, tanks and aircraft. The result was catastrophic. Writing of the scenes he witnessed in 1916, the poet Edmund Blunden wrote:

> Later that summer the battle of the Somme was fought, and men perished
> in great multitudes and in places where their bodies could not be recovered,
> so intense was the new artillery and machine-gun fire, so hopeless the mud

Opposite:
One of the most striking images from the First World War – these soldiers have become so inured to the devastation that they wash their hands in a shell crater that contains the remains of their comrades.

which went on for miles. The battalions who came up to the relief of those in the craters and vestiges of trenches would find themselves, in the fire-splashed night, stumbling over corpse after corpse. In deep dug-outs, twenty or thirty feet down, friends or foes were done to death by one means or another with the ultimate result that there was no entering those burnt-out, dreadful caverns.

'To realise fully the appalling high level of death and mutilation, one should also remember that the ratio of *fighting* soldiers to support troops was about one to five, so that statistically very few actual frontline men could escape at least some form of wound' (G. Kingsley Ward and Edwin Gibson in *Courage Remembered*).

Entrenchments stretched in a continuous line of opposing ditches from the North Sea coast of Belgium to the Swiss border, a distance of some 450 miles. A more unsuitable ground for trench warfare could hardly be imagined. Often there was only a thin layer of soil over non-porous clay, which meant that the trenches were slow to drain and during wet spells were feet deep in water and soon filled with sewage, debris and worse.

The war was fought not only on the Western Front but in Macedonia, Mesopotamia and East Africa. It was fought in Italy, in the Dardanelles, in Greece, in Palestine, and it was fought also on the seas. The British and German surface fleets fought four major sea battles, at Coronel, the Falklands, Dogger Bank and Jutland.

Into this situation stepped a man uniquely placed to interpret public opinion, to realise the needs and requirements of the Army, and with the connections to make a material difference on the ground. Neither a politician nor a soldier, Fabian Ware (1869–1949) was to found the Imperial (now Commonwealth) War Graves Commission, which today cares for the graves and memorials of over 1.7 million men and women of the two world wars. Ware had trained as a teacher and spent ten years as Assistant Director for

Major General Sir Fabian Ware CB CMG KCVO KBE (1869–1949), founder of the Imperial (now Commonwealth) War Graves Commission.

Education in the Transvaal from the mid-1890s and so had seen at first hand the gradual decay of the war cemeteries in South Africa. From 1905 Ware had been living in London, working first as the editor of the *Morning Post* and, from 1912, as an expert on educational reform. In 1914, at the age of forty-five and too old to fight, Ware volunteered to serve with the Red Cross in France. He had at that time no particular interest in the commemoration of the dead. His task was to take over a miscellaneous collection of cars and volunteer drivers who made up the Red Cross's mobile or 'flying' unit to bring the wounded to field hospitals and pick up stragglers who had lost their way.

Thousands of isolated burials appeared all over the Western Front during the early months of the First World War.

He also instructed his men to collect information on where the dead had been buried and to make careful note of precise locations. This was nothing out of the ordinary since the Red Cross saw it as one of its responsibilities to provide the next of kin with information about the burial sites of their sons, brothers or husbands. What was different was that the team became concerned about the state of the graves. It was clear to Ware that it was only a matter of time before families would make the journey to visit the burial

The care of soldiers' graves involved not only recording details but also caring for the temporary crosses on the graves.

sites of their lost men. He realised that their distress could be reduced if some care were taken over the graves.

In October 1914 Lieutenant Colonel Edward Stewart, a medical assessor for the Red Cross, came out to Lille to inspect the unit's work. Ware made a point of showing him a French cemetery at Béthune where several servicemen had been buried by their regiments. Each grave had a simple wooden cross. Stewart was impressed but was concerned by the temporary nature of the inscriptions, which had been made in pencil. He gave instructions that they should be painted on the reverse side of the cross, so as to avoid any mistakes. Furthermore he accepted that Ware should continue to record methodically the location and details of graves of British and Allied servicemen, and to care for their upkeep. This gave Ware's work increased focus and chimed with the growing sentiment in Britain that something had to be done about the graves of the fallen. *The Times* reported in January 1915 that a woman had been told where to find her brother's grave by his comrades but when she got to France she was distressed that she was unable to locate it.

By February 1915 Ware's unit had been officially recognised. Initially they were supported by the Red Cross but the Army provided rations, petrol and upkeep. Ware and his small team were also given military titles. Thus began what became his life's work. It was not always easy for Major General Ware's unit to gain access to the battle sites but he was aided by Major General Neville Macready, Adjutant-General to the British Expeditionary Force. He too had seen the neglected graves in South Africa and recognised the value of Ware's work to the Army's morale and did what he could to help. One of his contributions was to open negotiations to acquire land in the name of the French state for burial of Allied soldiers.

Sites for the cemeteries were chosen so as not to take up too much valuable agricultural land and to be a reasonable distance from housing. The French Government would then purchase the land from the owners and gift it, in perpetuity, to the British. Certain stipulations were laid down by the French, such as that the graves had to be placed 9–12 inches apart and a path not exceeding 3 feet wide was to be laid between the rows. This was the first of many pieces of the jigsaw puzzle that eventually came together as the template for an Imperial War Graves Commission cemetery.

Not everyone in Britain was happy with the idea of men being buried abroad and some prominent people argued for repatriation. Despite Marshall

Joffre's order of March 1915 banning exhumations for the period of the war, several wealthy families insisted on pursuing their objective. Ware determined to put a stop to it. He wrote: 'The one point of view that seems to me to be often overlooked in this matter is that of the officers themselves, who in ninety-nine cases out of a hundred will tell you that if they are killed they would wish to be among their men.' Macready issued an order forbidding exhumation on grounds of hygiene and 'on account of the difficulties of treating impartially the claims by persons of different social standing.' Ware wrote later: 'With the first glimmering of that spirit of democracy that was later to illumine the principles of the War Graves Commission came also a determination to do everything possible to supply consolation to the relatives of the dead.'

With the exception of some notable dissenters, the response to Macready's order from the general public at home was largely favourable and Ware's unit was almost overwhelmed with requests for information from relatives. When a grave was recorded, the family would receive a photograph of the cross with instructions on the accompanying card giving the best indication of the grave's location and even hints as to which railway station was closest to the site. So successful was the work in France and Belgium of the renamed Directorate of Graves Registration and Enquiries that it was extended to other theatres of war. There were units in Salonika (Thessaloniki) in Greece, in Egypt and in Mesopotamia (Iraq), and the work was carried out there with equal dedication.

The Commander-in-Chief of the Army, General (later Field Marshal) Sir Douglas Haig, wrote to the War Office in March 1915:

> It is fully recognised that the work of this organisation is of purely sentimental value, and that it does not directly contribute to the successful termination of the war. It has, however, an extraordinary moral value to the Troops in the Field as well as to the relatives and friends of the dead at home. The mere fact that these officers visit day after day, the cemeteries close behind the trenches, fully exposed to shell and rifle fire, accurately to record not only the names of the dead but also the exact place of burial, has a symbolic value to the men that it would be difficult to exaggerate.

By early 1917 Ware and his supporters, who included Major General Macready and the Prince of Wales, realised that a formal organisation would be needed to care for the cemeteries after the war was over. Initially the Office of Works, responsible for public buildings, parks and cemeteries, argued that it should be responsible, not least as it had under its remit the care of cemeteries in the Crimea and the Far East. Ware and Macready argued successfully that as the Empire had supplied hundreds of thousands of men to fight for the Allies

One fellow commissioner wrote of Kipling: 'I never met him without laughing, often at nothing in particular, really just because he was there with that look of "Let's have a lark' in his sparkling eyes.'

the organisation would have to be an Imperial one, with the member governments having a share of the responsibility for the development and continuity of work of the new body.

On 21 May 1917 the Imperial War Graves Commission was granted a Royal Charter. The Prince of Wales was to be its first President, and Lord Derby its Chairman; Ware was Vice-Chairman and Macready was also on the board; so too were the High Commissioners for Canada, Australia, New Zealand and South Africa, and India and Newfoundland were also represented. Sir William Garstin, the engineer of the Aswan Dam, was invited to become a Commissioner to add his weight to the already outstanding pool of artistic and horticultural expert advisers. Garstin had lost a son in the war. A further significant addition to the newly formed Commission was Rudyard Kipling, who was appointed literary adviser. He too had lost his only son, at Loos in September 1915.

The Imperial War Graves Commission was charged to care for all members of the Armed Forces of the British Empire who 'died from wounds inflicted, accident occurring or disease contracted, while on active service whether on sea or land'. It was empowered to acquire and hold land for cemeteries and for permanent memorials outside cemeteries. It was enjoined to provide for burials, to erect and care for memorials, to

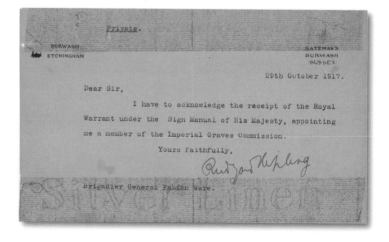

Kipling's letter agreeing to become a member of the Imperial War Graves Commission, dated October 1917, a month before the Commission's first meeting.

keep records and registers of the graves, and to look after those graves which lay outside cemeteries.

At the first meeting, held in November 1917, the major principles of the Commission were laid down and they still stand today. Macready expressed the view that 'in the erection of memorials on the graves there should be no distinction between officers and men.' This was a radical departure from the past, when officers were individually recognised whereas the ordinary soldier was, more often than not, put into a mass grave. Further, it was agreed that there should be no distinction between creed and nationality. Finally, Ware explained to the meeting that the cemeteries were to be constructed to last 'in perpetuity'. Never before had the ordinary man been accorded such respect and Ware was anxious to underline this:

> These dead deserved the honour which had been shown in this way to the
> former great of the earth, and as they could not be brought in their hundreds
> of thousands beneath the sacred shelter of existing monuments, structures
> at least as lasting must be erected at the spots in distant lands where their
> comrades buried them.

Brookwood Cemetery is the largest Commonwealth War Graves Commission cemetery in Britain and is the closest in its scale to the great cemeteries on the Western Front.

A WORLDWIDE TASK

Q UALIFICATION for burial in an Imperial War Graves cemetery after the
First World War was that a man or woman had to have been a member
of the armed services between 4 August 1914 and 31 August 1921. The reason
why the First World War period extends to 31 August 1921 for Commission
purposes is that the 'Termination of the Present War (Definition) Act' laid down
that the war would officially end when an Order in Council under that Act
declared the war ended. This duly occurred on 31 August 1921.

Burial of the dead was the responsibility of the Army, not of the Imperial
War Graves Commission, which was and remains responsible solely for the
cemeteries when they have been handed over by the Army. Although hundreds
of thousands of burials had taken place during the First World War, many
bodies were still scattered over the battlefields of the Western Front and had
to be brought in. In addition, there were thousands of isolated burials – men
interred hurriedly where they had fallen, or groups of half a dozen or so who
had been killed perhaps by a shell or in a gas attack. It was clear to the
Commission that it would be impossible to care for such tiny burial sites, and
for the French and Belgians it was also an issue for their farmers that valuable
agricultural land was pockmarked with individual burials. The Commission
was, however, aware of how strongly families felt that their men should remain
where they fell, so a carefully worded statement was published in the minutes
of the sixth meeting of the IWGC on 18 November 1918. It read:

> Over 150,000 such scattered graves are known in France and Belgium.
> In certain districts, notably those of Ypres and the Somme battlefields, they
> are thickly strewn over areas measuring several miles in length and breadth.
> These areas will shortly be restored to cultivation, or possibly afforested,
> and the bodies cannot remain undisturbed. They must therefore be removed
> to cemeteries where they can be reverently cared for. The Commission felt
> that any other course of action would be excessively painful to relatives and
> discreditable to the country and would place the cultivators of land
> throughout an enormous extent of territory in a most unfair position.

Opposite:
Maple Copse
Cemetery, in
Belgium, today
has the air of
an 'English
churchyard', as
Kenyon described
in his report in
1918.

21

Both these men, who were killed in action in 1919, are commemorated on Face 23 on the Delhi Memorial (India Gate), one of 13,313 names recorded on Lutyens's monument.

Sometimes, as here at the Royal Berkshire Military Cemetery, it was possible for a regiment to keep its own cemetery but more often than not, in the chaos of the battles, men had to be buried where they fell.

It was a delicate topic and the Commission took Macready's advice that where possible a little unit of ten graves might be used to form the nucleus of a larger so-called concentration cemetery. One of the most famous examples of this is Tyne Cot, now the Commission's largest cemetery, holding nearly twelve thousand burials, of which over three-quarters are unidentified. The original battlefield cemetery at Tyne Cot, which also served as a local dressing station during the war, had just forty-eight burials.

Between the Armistice of 11 November 1918 and September 1921 the Graves Concentration Units carried out systematic searches, taking 204,650 bodies from battlefields and reburying them in cemeteries set aside to receive them. Every clue found on a body, however apparently insignificant, was used in an attempt to identify the remains. A very tall man or one with a distinctive tattoo might just provide enough evidence for him to be identified by his regiment. The members of the Graves Concentration Units became detectives *par excellence* and acquired an unrivalled knowledge of the particular shades of khaki issued to any unit at any time.

Private John McCauley worked for an exhumation company in 1919. He wrote: 'For the first week or two I could scarcely endure the experience we met with, but I gradually became hardened.'

Burial Returns were produced by the Graves Concentration Units when they did battlefield clearance work after the First World War.

'Exhumation was a routine job despite its grimness,' one Australian wrote. 'The grave would be opened and the body uncovered. The body was checked for identity discs, paybooks, papers or anything else that could be used in identification. Then the body was wrapped in a blanket, sewn up and

CONCENTRATION OF GRAVES (Exhumation and Reburials).

BURIAL RETURN.

Name of Cemetery of Reburial LONDON CEM.EXTN., High Wood, LONGUEVAL. 57c.S.4.c.9.5.

Plot	Row	Grave	Map Reference where body found	Was cross on grave?	Regimental particulars	Means of Identification	Were any effects forwarded to Base?
1.	A.	9.	57d.A.6.a.95.15.	No.	UNKNOWN BRITISH SOLDIER, Seaforth Hldrs.	0.S.tunic,kilt, boots,titles.	Titles.
1.	A.	10.	57d.A.6.a.9.2.	No.	UNKNOWN BRITISH OFFICER, Gn Seron Hldrs.	Officer's tunic, kilt,buttons. Spec.Ex.Report	Buttons. Ring marked inside M.K Piece belt stamped CAM. 279.
1.	A.	11.	57c.S.1.d.25.90.	No.	UNKNOWN BRITISH SOLDIER.	0.S.uniform, & buttons.	No.
1.	A.	12.	57c.S.1.d.1.7.	No.	UNKNOWN BRITISH SOLDIER.	0.S.uniform, boots.	No.
1.	A.	13.	57d.A.6.a.80.25.	No.	UNKNOWN BRITISH SOLDIER, Black Watch.	0.S.tunic,kilt, boots,titles.	Titles.
1.	A.	14.	57d.A.6.a.75.25.	No.	UNKNOWN BRITISH SOLDIER.	0.S.uniform, boots.	Piece repaired boot stamped 7 B-, 468. Piece equipment stamped 87. Piece P.sheet marked--,19
1.	A.	15.	-do-	No.	UNKNOWN BRITISH SOLDIER.	0.S.uniform,boots.	Denture marked 4286.
1.	A.	16.	-do-	No.	UNKNOWN BRITISH SOLDIER.	0.S.uniform, boots.	Piece equipment stamped B-,-1911.
1.	A.	17.	-do-	No.	UNKNOWN BRITISH SOLDIER.	0.S.uniform, boots.	No.

This form to be made out in triplicate, two copies being handed to the D.A.D. G.R. of G.R.C.

marked with an identifying tag for future occasions.' The body was then moved to the designated cemetery and buried with formality and dignity. A temporary wooden cross was erected above the grave and inscribed with the religion, regimental number, rank, name, unit and date of death.

Having established the simple but remarkably forward-looking principles of equality of rank, creed and race, the Commission's next task was to find an outline design for the construction of a cemetery. The challenge was to produce a template that would allow individual architects freedom to express their own ideas and interpret individual sites while adhering to a basic set of uniform principles. To this end they appointed Lieutenant Colonel Sir Frederic Kenyon, the Director of the British Museum, to be the Commission's artistic adviser. This was a brilliant appointment because Kenyon was not only well travelled and widely respected within the artistic establishment but he had the authority of having served with the Inns of Court Regiment during the war.

In July 1917 Ware had sent the architects Sir Edwin Lutyens and Herbert Baker with the Director of the Tate Gallery, Charles Aitken, to France to see

Cassino War Cemetery in Italy was laid out after the Second World War. It shows how Kenyon's artistic vision of 1918 stood the test of time.

for themselves the terrible sights of the battlefields and to return with some recommendations. Not only had they been unable to agree on an approach when they were in France but on their return they were even less in agreement as to what was to be done. Lutyens, deeply disturbed by what he had seen, advocated an abstract approach to design whereas Baker wanted to make the cross central to the cemeteries. Aitken was against extravagance and favoured spending on social housing and benefits at home. Kenyon was to broker peace and offer his own artistic vision. He did so at the Commission's second meeting in February 1918 and his vision for the cemeteries was so simple and clear that it has stood the test of time.

Given that what confronted Kenyon was not the green and pleasant hills of the Somme and Passchendaele that we see today but rather an alien landscape torn to pieces and blasted by the ravages of a war of such gargantuan destruction as to defy imagination, it is all the more remarkable that what he described is so close to what now exists. He wrote:

> The general appearance of a British cemetery will be that of an enclosure with plots of grass or flowers (or both) separated by paths of varying size, and set with orderly rows of headstones, uniform in height and width. Shrubs and trees will be arranged in various places, sometimes as clumps at the junctions of ways, sometimes as avenues along the sides of the principal paths, sometimes around the borders of the cemetery. The graves will, wherever possible, face towards the east, and at the eastern end of the cemetery will be a great altar stone, raised upon broad steps, and bearing some brief and appropriate phrase or text. Either over the stone, or elsewhere in the cemetery, will be a small building, where visitors may gather for shelter or for worship, and where the register of the graves will be kept. And at some prominent spot will rise the Cross, as the symbol of the Christian faith and of the self-sacrifice of the men who now lie beneath its shadow.

The great altar stone he referred to was to be designed by Lutyens, who had sketched it out on the back of an envelope in France. He had described: 'One great fair stone of fine proportions, twelve feet in length, lying raised upon three steps, of which the first and third shall be twice the width of the second.' This became known as the Stone of Remembrance and was inscribed with words from Ecclesiastes, chosen by Kipling: 'Their name liveth for evermore.' It had the advantage in its abstract form of ambiguity. For those who wish it, the stone can be interpreted as an altar. For those who eschew specific religious associations, it stands simply as an object of remembrance.

The Cross of Sacrifice, designed by Sir Reginald Blomfield, was overtly Christian and reflected the majority religion of the time. The bronze sword that adorns the cross reminds the visitor of the military nature of the war cemeteries.

Maple Copse outside Ypres c.1917. 'In the clash and bewilderment of actual fighting, in the rapid ruin and chaos and oblivion of the front line with its enormous process of annihilation, perhaps not many soldiers retained the confidence that the dead – themselves, it might be, tomorrow or the next instant – would at length obtain some lasting and distinct memorial'. (Edmund Blunden).

Five Crosses of Sacrifice are visible in this now peaceful landscape of the Somme.

Blomfield allowed the Cross of Sacrifice to be reproduced to scale in four different sizes so that almost every cemetery could have a cross. Lutyens was adamant that the Stone of Remembrance, however, was not to be scaled down and thus in theory only cemeteries with more than a thousand burials have one, though there are cemeteries on the Western Front that are exceptions. Another exception is Botley Cemetery in Oxford, which has 741 identified graves. It was an important cemetery in both world wars. During the First World War the 3rd Southern General Hospital (an Oxfordshire Territorial unit) was housed

in the Examination Schools and a number of other buildings in Oxford. In the Second World War Botley Cemetery was designated a Royal Air Force regional cemetery. There are 156 First and 516 Second World War burials as well as seventy burials of other nationalities, including Germans, Poles, Italians and French.

So began the work of the Commission, to construct cemeteries and memorials to bury and commemorate the 1.1 million servicemen of the Empire who had died in the First World War. It was a task that Kipling described as 'the biggest single bit of work since the Pharaohs and they only worked in their own country.' The handing over of cemeteries by the War Office Directorate to the Commission in France and Belgium began in 1920

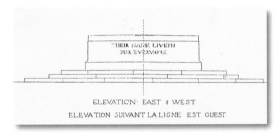

An early sketch by Lutyens of the Stone of Remembrance.

Buttes New British Cemetery, near Zonnebeke in West Flanders, was designed by Charles Holden. It qualifies for a Stone of Remembrance as it has over two thousand burials, though only 431 are identified.

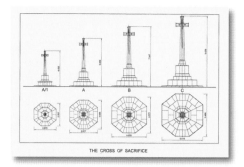

THE CROSS OF SACRIFICE

Blomfield designed the Cross of Sacrifice so that it could be scaled up or down to fit more than one size of cemetery.

Suda Bay War Cemetery on Crete, with its cross dominating the bay, was created after the Second World War.

and by February 1921 the Commission had responsibility for 2,400 cemeteries and the records of 1,400 of these had been certified, checked and passed to the Commission. Once the handover had taken place, the cemetery was surveyed in order to furnish the French or Belgian authorities with the information requisite for the acquisition of the land. On the basis of this survey, one of the principal architects, Lutyens, Blomfield or Baker, would then propose a general design that was elaborated by the staff of architects on the spot. While this was being done, the cemetery was placed in the charge of the horticultural department, which would develop a planting plan in consultation with the architect.

A colossal task in the early days was the manufacture of the nearly half a million headstones. Opposition to the design of the headstone was loud in certain quarters and the matter of headstone versus cross was eventually debated in the House of Commons. The main argument that the Commission put forward was, as usual, one of practicality. There would be more space on a headstone for the regimental badge and personal inscription, to be chosen by the family, whereas on the cross space was more limited. The Commission's view was finally upheld.

The headstones were to be of a uniform shape and size – 2 feet 6 inches high, 1 foot 3 inches wide and 3 inches thick – with emphasis on simplicity

and clear lettering to keep down both production costs and future maintenance. Portland stone and Hopton Wood limestone were recommended by the Geological Museum in London. The qualities of these stones meant they were cheap, durable and local. The shape of the headstone was once again chosen on practical as well as aesthetic grounds. The gentle rounding of the top helped to disperse the rain and stop water pouring down the front face of the headstone. The lettering was recommended by Macdonald Gill, the brother of the sculptor Eric Gill, to a committee that comprised directors of the Wallace Collection and the National Gallery. It was designed so that it could be read at a 45-degree angle from above and from the side, so that visitors did not have to kneel down and could scan a line of headstones for a name. The choice of Roman lettering was deemed to be suitably sober as well as clear and easy to read.

Tyne Cot Cemetery has nearly twelve thousand headstones, three-quarters of which read: 'A Soldier of the Great War. Known Unto God.'

The issue of engraving regimental badges, each of which it was estimated would take one skilled craftsman a week to carve, was eventually solved by a Lancashire firm. They invented a machine called a pantograph that could trace the patterns of the regimental badges and inscriptions onto the stone. This worked successfully and the company manufactured fifty thousand headstones in the first five years. Between 1920 and 1923 more than four thousand headstones were shipped to France each week.

A standard Commission headstone for an outstanding man: Captain Noel Godfrey Chavasse VC and Bar, MC is the only holder of the Victoria Cross and Bar from the First World War and one of only three men to have been awarded this distinction. His is the only headstone in the world to have two Victoria Crosses engraved upon it.

Headstone production in the 1920s reached record levels, with up to four thousand a week being shipped to France.

While all this was happening on the Western Front, activity in Italy, Turkey and the Middle East was also under way. Sir Robert Lorimer was appointed chief architect for Italy and Greece. His rustic designs for the cemeteries high up on the Asiago plateau, where the gardener inspects his sites on skis for most of the winter, were praised by Ware for being some of the most beautiful of all the Commission's cemeteries. In Italy the headstones were carved from Chiampo Perla limestone. This limestone was available locally and it fitted in well with the landscape, but another consideration was the outstanding quality of the Italian stonemasons. At all junctures the Commission was far-sighted enough to opt for local or simple solutions where they would work best.

Further afield still, the Scottish architect John James Burnet was given the task of building cemeteries and memorials in Palestine and on the Gallipoli peninsula. The latter presented the Commission with an especial problem since the Allies had not set foot on the peninsula since their withdrawal in

Forli Indian Army War Cemetery in Italy. A rose planted between each pair of marble headstones and other low shrubs and perennials give colour and interest for much of the year.

1915, so that, although the regiments had buried their dead and marked the graves, much had been lost to the ravages of weather and time.

If constructing cemeteries in France and Belgium was difficult because of the sheer numbers of burials then the problems at Gallipoli were magnified by the remoteness of the peninsula and the difficulty of getting materials to sites that during the war had been approached from the sea. In 1919 the Australian and New Zealand governments offered to take over the work of construction at Gallipoli in view of the numbers of their soldiers who died there. They undertook much of the necessary preliminary work, such as repairing roads and constructing a railway from the quarry, before Burnet could visit and propose his designs.

This is the sight at Shell Green that confronted the Army on its return to Gallipoli in 1919 after an absence of four years.

Today Shell Green Cemetery has 409 First World War burials, eleven of them unidentified.

The cemeteries in the Dardanelles are an excellent example of the Commission's ideas interpreted to suit the environment, where winter blizzards rip across the peninsula but summer temperatures can rise to 36°C. The entire ANZAC area has been preserved as a memorial to the men who died there in 1915, so that the battlegrounds are preserved alongside the cemeteries with their evocative names: Johnson's Jolly, Shrapnel Valley, Lone Pine and Plugge's Plateau. There are twenty-one cemeteries and three memorials within one mile or so of the beach at ANZAC Cove, a strong visual reminder of the intensity of the fighting in 1915 and of the ferocious opposition the Allied forces met from the Turkish troops defending the peninsula.

At Gallipoli the burial places of the unknown casualties are marked on cemetery plans but not on the ground. This gives the cemeteries a different feel from the silent cities of the Western Front, for wide expanses of open space are dotted with a small number of low grave markers. Pedestal stones were used rather than headstones as the ground was too unstable to take the horizontal beams in which the headstones sit and these have further added to Gallipoli's special character.

Burnet succeeded in capturing the mood of the landscape in his treatment of the cemeteries and memorials and there is a harmony here that

The Australians and New Zealanders who returned to Gallipoli in 1919 provided basic infrastructure. A railway line leads into a quarry, where the stone for the pedestals was carved.

Canterbury Cemetery photographed in March 2006 by Brian Harris. This brief covering of snow soon evaporated in the mid-morning sun.

Ware, in the foreground here at Beach Cemetery, visited Gallipoli in the 1920s to examine the Commission's work.

Beach Cemetery was used from the day of landing at ANZAC almost until the evacuation. In the centre of the cemetery the graves are randomly placed, typical of a battlefield cemetery, but the graves on either side are set in straight lines as order was restored.

renders it a remarkable place. It is now the focus for the 25 April ANZAC Day celebrations and thousands of visitors arrive for the ceremony each year.

One of the most important aspects of the Commission's work was the horticultural treatment of the cemeteries. Kenyon had stipulated the use of shrubs, trees and flowers but it was left to Lutyens's friend Gertrude Jekyll to be more specific about exactly how a cemetery should be laid out. Although her plans and designs were not adopted wholesale, there is no doubt that her influence was felt in the horticultural planning, not least in her suggestion that a rose should be planted between each pair of headstones so that the names would be shaded by an English rose. The horticulturalists worked hand in hand with the architects in the early days so as to come up with plans that would 'be simple and compatible with the dignity of the work'. The overall effect aimed at was to imitate an

Beach Cemetery in Gallipoli, photographed in 2006. The battlefield headstones are visible at the top of the picture.

Lone Pine Memorial commemorates more than 4,900 Australian and New Zealand servicemen who died in the ANZAC area and whose graves are not known, or who died in the waters off the peninsula.

The English rose grows in all but the harshest of conditions.

old-fashioned English churchyard with swathes of neatly cropped grass and mixed borders of flowers and shrubs to soften the architecture and the rows of headstones.

During the war and immediately afterwards graves had been decorated with local wild flowers. The scarlet poppy, which became the enduring symbol of remembrance, grows best in freshly turned soil and as a result had sprung up in huge numbers all over the battlefields of France and Belgium, adding a blast of colour to the devastated landscape. 'There was a wild profusion – beautiful it was – of wild flowers – poppies, cornflowers, white camomile and yellow charlock,' recalled Captain J. S. Parker, one of the Commission's first two horticultural officers, 'and we supplemented those with a few annuals, just to brighten up the borders.'

Further afield the horticultural teams had to be inventive and use local plants that would survive in the prevalent climate but it is surprising how hardy the English rose turned out to be and it grows in all but the harshest of environments.

Under the terms of its charter, the Imperial War Graves Commission was entitled 'to acquire a limited amount of land in the UK for cemeteries and offices', as well as building permanent memorials as needed. It is

perhaps a surprising statistic but over half of the Commission's burial sites, some twelve thousand, are in the United Kingdom. The main reason for this is that men who were injured and died later of their wounds, or of disease or accident while they were serving and before the official cut-off dates, were entitled to a Commission headstone. Some are sited individually within churches and graveyards, whereas elsewhere there are dedicated plots or whole cemeteries. The largest Commission cemetery in Britain is Brookwood Military Cemetery in Surrey, which contains the graves of over five thousand service men and women in 37 acres of grounds. There are 2,400 Canadian graves at Brookwood and 3,500 names are commemorated on the Brookwood Memorial. It is only at the large, exclusively war graves plots, such as at Brookwood and the RAF regional cemeteries at Bath, Cambridge, Harrogate, Chester and Oxford, that the Commission has been able fully to express that spirit of unity which characterises its work abroad. Only 416 of the United Kingdom sites are large enough to have a Cross of Sacrifice and there are thirteen Stones of Remembrance in Britain, two of which are at Brookwood, which also has two Crosses of Sacrifice. This is unique among the Commission cemeteries worldwide and is on account of the layout at Brookwood.

In the Second World War Botley Cemetery was designated a Royal Air Force regional cemetery. There are 156 First and 516 Second World War burials as well as seventy burials of other nationalities including Germans, Poles, Italians and French.

1914-1918

IN HONOUR OF THE NAVY
AND TO THE ABIDING MEMORY
OF THESE RANKS AND
RATINGS OF THIS PORT WHO LAID DOWN
THEIR LIVES IN THE DEFENCE OF THE EMPIRE AND
HAVE NO OTHER GRAVE THAN THE SEA

1939-1945

MEMORIALS TO THE MISSING AND THE SECOND WORLD WAR

O NE OF THE biggest problems Sir Frederic Kenyon identified in 1918 was the thousands of isolated burials:

> ... men buried hastily where they fell, men buried by the shell or mine explosion which killed them, men whose bodies could not be reached at the time for burial and who would have been subsequently sought out and buried by the devoted labour of the officers and men of the Directorate ... Many bodies are found but cannot be identified; many are never found at all; many are buried in graves which have subsequently been destroyed in the course of the fighting. This is especially the case in areas such as that of Ypres, where the same ground has been contested for three consecutive years, and the whole countryside has been blasted and torn with shell fire. Therefore whatever may be done in the way of placing individual monuments over the dead, in very many cases no such monument is possible. Yet these must not be neglected, and some memorial there must be to the lost, the unknown, but not forgotten dead.

These men, he suggested, should be commemorated on monuments close to the area where they were known to have fallen.

As nearly half the men who died in the First World War had no known grave and the Commission was committed to its principle of commemorating every man by name, a solution for the missing had to be found. At first the Commissioners were against the idea of associating the names of the missing with particular battles. However, in view of the enormous numbers involved and the need to limit the amount of land requested from the French and Belgian governments in particular, it was finally decided to commemorate the names on campaign monuments.

The monuments to the missing gave the architects an opportunity to express in their own style the enormity of the human sacrifice of the War. Each interpreted the loss differently: Baker looked to ancient Rome for his inspiration, Blomfield to simple, classical forms and Lutyens to the abstract.

Opposite:
The monumental Portsmouth Naval Memorial was designed by Sir Robert Lorimer. It commemorates some ten thousand sailors of the First World War and almost fifteen thousand of the Second World War.

A list of men commemorated on a panel in Bay One of the Arras Memorial, recording fourteen names out of nearly 35,000.

The Menin Gate Memorial at Ypres is now the focus of a moving ceremony of remembrance that takes place each evening at 8 p.m., at which Last Post is sounded.

The first of the great monuments to be commissioned was the Menin Gate Memorial at Ypres. In July 1919 the Belgian government agreed that the Menin Gate and the Ramparts should remain in their ruined state until the British came up with a scheme to turn them into a national memorial. The site of the gate was chosen because hundreds of thousands of Allied servicemen had passed through it on their way to the battlefields of the Ypres Salient between 1914 and 1918. Blomfield worked on the designs for this memorial during the summer of 1922 and in early 1923 the contract was granted. King George V, on his pilgrimage to visit the cemeteries of France and Belgium in May 1922, stopped at Ypres and discussed the plans for the memorial with Blomfield.

The solution that Blomfield came up with was essentially a classical barrel-vaulted structure lit by three unglazed openings reminiscent of the Pantheon in Rome. It is neither triumphal nor celebratory but there is an impressive permanence that neither

Above: King George V made a pilgrimage to France and Belgium in May 1922 to visit the 'Silent Cities'. To this end he required a passport, which was issued for just nine days.

Left: The Menin Gate Memorial was the first of the Commission's monuments to the missing to be unveiled on the Western Front.

While he was on his pilgrimage to France and Belgium, King George V discussed the designs for the Menin Gate Memorial with Blomfield (wearing a velvet collar).

Over 55,000 names of men missing in the Ypres Salient area are recorded on the Menin Gate Memorial at Ypres.

glorifies war nor applauds victory. The Menin Gate Memorial was completed in 1927 and unveiled by Field Marshal Lord Plumer in July of that year. The names of some 55,000 men are commemorated on 160 panels but that represented only a fraction of the missing from the Ypres Salient. Eventually six memorials were constructed in Belgium to commemorate these men, including Baker's magnificent stone and flint memorial at Tyne Cot Cemetery.

The memorial to the missing of the Somme was to be the largest of the Commission's memorials in the world. A site on a ridge overlooking the

Sir Herbert Baker's memorial at Tyne Cot Cemetery commemorates 34,900 men who died in the Ypres Salient and who have no known grave.

Thiepval commemorates the names of 72,000 men missing on the Somme.

Ancre was chosen and Lutyens was commissioned to build what has become recognised as one of his most imaginative turns of genius. The brick and stone memorial, with its massive square pillars and its enormous arches, commemorates the names of more than 72,000 officers and men who died on the Somme but have no known grave. Its dominating presence in the landscape serves as a permanent reminder of the dreadful losses. 'To describe the Thiepval Memorial as an "Arch" is a simplification,' wrote the architectural historian Gavin Stamp; 'marginally bigger than the Arc de Triomphe, it is no triumphal arch but a form of the greatest intellectual

The memorial to the Missing of the Somme at Thiepval, designed by Sir Edwin Lutyens, stands on a hill above the Ancre overlooking the battlefields of the Somme.

The unveiling ceremony of The Helles Memorial on Gallipoli. It bears the names of over 21,000 men who died in operations throughout the peninsula or were buried at sea in Gallipoli waters.

Two lions on the naval memorial at Chatham designed by the sculptor Sir Henry Poole.

complexity which, by its sublime massing and poignant openness, directly conveys a sense of the eternally tragic.' The inscription on the memorial reads simply 'To the Memory of the Missing of the Somme'.

Away from the Western Front, memorials were required in places where battles had been fought and men lost without trace. Sir Robert Lorimer designed a memorial to the missing in Salonika, a severe monument at Lake Doiran that marks the scene of the fierce fighting of 1917–18, which caused the majority of the Commonwealth battle casualties in that campaign.

At Gallipoli Burnet designed the Helles Memorial, an enormous pylon over 100 feet high, standing on high ground about Cape Helles and visible to all ships entering the Dardanelles. The names of the ships and military units that took part in the Gallipoli campaign are inscribed on the monument alongside the names of over twenty thousand men carved on walls around the monolith. Burnet designed two further memorials, at the Jerusalem War Cemetery in Israel, with its memorial chapel, and the Memorial to the Missing Indians at Port Tewfik in Egypt. This was destroyed in the Arab–Israeli War of 1967 and the names of those commemorated at Port Tewfik are now inscribed on the Heliopolis (Port Tewfik) Memorial outside Cairo. One of the largest memorials in the Middle East was erected at Basra and records the names of over forty thousand servicemen who died in operations in Mesopotamia between 1914 and 1921 and have no known grave. Owing to the sensitivity of the area around the naval dockyard where it stood, the memorial was moved in 1997 by presidential decree to a site 32 km away.

Given its independent and unique burial traditions, the Navy was not initially inclined to feel it came under the umbrella of the Imperial War Graves Commission. In 1918 the Commission learned that the Admiralty had plans to erect a monument to all those lost at sea. The Commissioners felt it was their duty to commemorate all those whose lives had been lost in the First World War, not just those who had fought on land, and eventually they agreed to erect memorials at Portsmouth, Plymouth and Chatham – the Royal Navy's three manning ports.

Sir Robert Lorimer proposed 'a grey granite tower supported by four corner buttresses each with a lion *couchant*. Towards the top, the tower branched out in the form of four ships' prows. Above them were the representations of the four winds, which in turn supported a large copper sphere symbolising the globe.' In the end the Plymouth memorial was given extra height and these three memorials commemorate all the British seamen and some of the South Africans and Australians.

The names of those soldiers who lost their lives at sea were inscribed in cemeteries nearest to their last point of embarkation and the most notable of these was the Hollybrook Memorial at Southampton, which has the names of two thousand soldiers including Lord Kitchener, who perished in HMS *Hampshire* in 1915. Merchant seamen have their own memorial at Tower Hill in London designed by Lutyens, and this monument was extended after the Second World War to commemorate the names of those lost at sea between 1939 and 1945. It is the only naval memorial to have a Stone of Remembrance.

After 1945 the naval memorials too were extended to accommodate the names of those who had been lost at sea in the Second World War. Sir Edward Maufe, who had been appointed to succeed Sir Frederic Kenyon as the

The Tower Hill Memorial in London, designed by Sir Edwin Lutyens, commemorates almost 36,000 members of the Merchant Navy and fishing fleets from both wars.

Commission's artistic adviser, was also its lead architect. Not only did he design the extensions to the naval memorials but he also created a new and very handsome memorial to the Royal Air Force at Runnymede in Surrey, overlooking the River Thames. It commemorates over twenty thousand men and women who died in operations over northern Europe and who have no known grave. Of all the work created by Maufe, the Royal Air Force Memorial is undoubtedly his finest. It was unveiled in October 1953 by the newly crowned Queen Elizabeth II.

The far-flung theatres of the 1939–45 war demanded new solutions and the Commission had to rise to the challenge of creating cemeteries and memorials in remote and often inhospitable parts of the world. One of the largest was at El Alamein in Egypt, where seven thousand men are buried in the cemetery designed by Sir Hubert Worthington and over 8,500 soldiers and three thousand airmen are commemorated on the Alamein Memorial. When Worthington visited Africa in 1943 he declared that, although he would follow the brief to build and plant along the same lines as the cemeteries from the First World War, the climate and environment in Africa would require modifications. He suggested high walls to keep out drifting sands and shady pergolas and cool terraces to provide shelter from the sun. Where grass could not be grown, owing to the lack of water, the earth would

Designed by Sir Edward Maufe and unveiled by Queen Elizabeth II on 17 October 1953, the Runnymede Memorial, on a hill above the River Thames, commemorates the names of over twenty thousand men and women who were lost in operations over Europe between 1939 and 1945.

This photograph, taken soon after burials were completed in El Alamein War Cemetery, shows how difficult a task it was to provide a horticultural scheme for Egypt.

have to be panned, and such plants as succulents and cacti would be used rather than the thirsty roses and shrubs grown in Europe and other parts of the world.

The Singapore Memorial at Kranji holds the names of over 24,000 servicemen who died, some in the fight for Singapore and others during the three and a half years of captivity at the hands of the Japanese. The largest memorial in south-east Asia is at Taukkyan War Cemetery in Rangoon, where the memorial records the names of over 26,000 men who died in Burma and have no known grave. In total over 759,000 names are commemorated on the Commission's memorials from both world wars.

Twelve thousand Allied prisoners of the Japanese died during the construction of the Thailand–Burma Railway, mostly from disease

Sir Hubert Worthington worked with rather than against the landscape and produced an ordered cemetery with sparse but careful planting in a tough environment.

Chungkai War Cemetery was started by prisoners of war at a base hospital camp on the Thailand–Burma Railway. Most of the men buried here died at the hospital while being treated for disease and injuries sustained during the construction of the railway.

The original register for Sai Wan Cemetery in Hong Kong describes the magnificent view of the harbour.

and neglect. These men's remains are held in three war cemeteries, Thanbyuzayat in Burma and Chungkai and Kanchanaburi in Thailand. During the war the men had been buried close to the camps where they died, but the bodies were gathered in 1946 and the remains concentrated into the three cemeteries that exist today. Generally the policy after the Second World War was to make greater use of concentration cemeteries in order to minimise the amount of land taken out of use and to help keep

Designed by Colin St Clair Oakes, this beautiful terraced cemetery at Kohima in India is one of the loveliest of all the Second World War sites. It was here that this inscription first appeared: 'When you go home, Tell them of us and say, For your tomorrow, We gave our today.'

the number of cemeteries in far-flung regions to manageable numbers. Colin St Clair Oakes designed the war cemeteries in the Far East and, as at Gallipoli, there was risk of earthquake so he adopted the pedestal headstone, this time with a bronze plaque. His beautiful cemetery at Kohima in northern India, erected on the battleground of Garrison Hill, is probably one of the most evocative of the Second World War sites in Asia.

The view of Hong Kong harbour is now all but obliterated by the skyscrapers that crowd around the cemetery's perimeter.

COMMEMORATION OF THE WAR DEAD SINCE 1945

A S WITH THE First World War, the cut-off date for the Second World War for burials in Commission cemeteries was extended, this time to eighteen months after the end of hostilities. Thereafter the cemeteries were closed to new burials and the Ministry of Defence is now responsible for Forces' cemeteries in the post-Second World War era. From July 1950 Britain was involved in the Korean War but although Australia and Canada also took part, the war did not engage a full Commonwealth force so a new Imperial War Graves Commission cemetery was not built. Out of the 81,000 British servicemen, from all three forces, who fought in that war, 1,335 died, of whom 885 are buried in the United Nations Memorial Cemetery Korea (UNMCK) at Pusan. Of the remainder, some bodies were never found so those men are commemorated on the Commonwealth Memorial at UNMCK, while 44 are buried in the post-war section of the Commission's cemetery in Hodogaya, Japan, where they had been hospital patients.

The Ministry of Defence (MoD) and the Commonwealth War Graves Commission, renamed in 1960 to reflect the changing times, work closely in alliance on many burial sites. In 1982 the MoD requested the Commission

The United Nations Memorial Cemetery in Seoul was established in January 1951 and dedicated four months later.

50

to design and construct a cemetery and memorial, to be called Blue Beach, at San Carlos on the Falkland Islands to take the dead of the 1982 Falklands War. Lieutenant Colonel H. Jones VC is buried in Blue Beach Cemetery, which was unveiled on 10 April 1983. Of the 255 who died, sixteen are buried on the Falkland Islands, 174 have no grave but the sea, and sixty-four servicemen's remains were repatriated to the United Kingdom.

For some time the question of repatriation of remains versus familial involvement in funeral services abroad was under consideration. On 14 March 1963 the Secretary of State for War, John Profumo, announced in the House of Commons that he had been in discussion with the Minister of Defence and members of the armed services about the question of service burial: 'We have looked at two possible measures: bringing home the dead where relatives so wish, or, alternatively, flying out two relatives to the funeral.' Given the logistical problems of distance and burial practicalities they decided that the policy of the next of kin choosing to bring the body home at public expense for private burial or having two relatives flown out to attend the service funeral could apply only to northern Europe, and only as circumstances permitted. Nevertheless this was a major change and it was followed four years later to the day with a statement by the minister then responsible, Merlyn Rees, to the effect that the policy was to be extended beyond northern Europe but only to countries where it was practicable and safe.

However, it was not until March 2003 that the whole question of the repatriation of remains was made official. From that point on, service personnel who die in the course of operations or their duties abroad are repatriated to the United Kingdom at the expense of the Ministry of Defence. The office responsible for this work is the Joint Casualty and

Blue Beach Cemetery at San Carlos on the Falkland Islands contains the remains of fourteen servicemen from the Falklands War.

Since 2003 the remains of service personnel killed abroad are repatriated. A respectful tradition of lining the streets to honour the dead began in the Wiltshire town of Wootton Bassett.

Compassionate Cell, which deals with practical details and advises families on procedures and entitlements, and offers support where it can. The repatriation ceremony at RAF Lyneham in Wiltshire is a formal military occasion to which the family of the deceased is invited. Thereafter, following the post-mortem, the coffin is handed over to the family, and the decisions over all funeral arrangements are left to the family, who may or may not wish to invite military personnel to attend. In addition, the family can opt for a service headstone, which the MoD will maintain in perpetuity, or they can choose their own design, in which case the family assumes responsibility for the future upkeep.

The Armed Forces Memorial, designed by Liam O'Connor, is dedicated to the men and women of the United Kingdom Armed Forces killed on duty or as a result of terrorist action since the Second World War.

This sculptural group 'The Stretcher Bearers' by Ian Rank-Broadley at the Armed Forces Memorial draws on the story of the death of Patroclus, the hero whose body was carried back to camp held aloft on Achilles' shield, having impersonated Achilles by borrowing his armour.

Although war cemeteries are no longer being created either in conflict zones or in Britain there is nevertheless a desire on the part of the public to commemorate those who die in the course of their duty to their country. As a result, a memorial has been created at the National Memorial Arboretum in Staffordshire to commemorate over sixteen thousand servicemen and women who have died since 1945. The Armed Forces Memorial is the work of the Irish architect Liam O'Connor and is in the same proud tradition as the First World War memorials of Lutyens, Baker and Blomfield. Neither triumphal nor glorifying war, it is nevertheless a majestic composition that combines humility at the cost of human sacrifice with the honour and pride of serving in the armed forces. The memorial is augmented by two outstanding sculptural groups by Ian Rank-Broadley, whose realistic figures step out of the tradition of C. S. Jagger, Frances Derwent-Wood and Gilbert Ledward, who were all called to respond in their art to the horrors of the First World War. Thus the focus of commemoration has shifted away from war cemeteries and back to memorials, though the emphasis on remembering each individual without regard to race, rank or creed, as suggested by General Macready in November 1917, has become universally accepted.

This figure on the Armed Forces Memorial by Ian Rank-Broadley is poised as if to carve the inscription 'We Will Remember Them Today, Tomorrow and For Ever'.

AN UNCHANGING TASK IN A CHANGING WORLD

A N UNEXPECTED side-effect of the Commission's war cemeteries all over the world is that they mark the sites of historical battles and struggles. Not only do they serve as a reminder of the terrible losses of the two world wars but they also help to lift history from the pages of a book and make it relevant for visitors to the cemeteries and memorials, few of whom any longer have a direct association with those buried beneath the headstones.

The Commonwealth War Graves Commission is charged with the care of its cemeteries and memorials in perpetuity. Many challenges face the horticultural and architectural experts, including climate change, subsidence, storms, earthquakes and, of course, new wars. Since 2003 it has not been possible for the Commission to look after its cemeteries and memorials in Iraq and it is known that they are in a state of disrepair. In 2008 the Commission opened a Book of Remembrance at its headquarters in Maidenhead that records the names of all those buried and commemorated in Iraq from the First and Second World Wars. The pages are turned daily. However, the Commission can afford to take a long view and in due course it will be possible to reconstruct the cemeteries and memorials from the plans and records that have been carefully kept.

Such a project has already been carried out. Zehrensdorf Indian Cemetery was situated in former East Germany and was for a long time in the Russian zone in an area where the Soviet forces conducted target practice. As the Commission was unable to maintain the cemetery during this period, the casualties were instead commemorated by name on special panels erected at the Indian memorial at Neuve-Chapelle in France. After the reunification of Germany in 1990, the Commission could return to the site and rebuild the cemetery, replace headstones and install a new Stone of Remembrance. The cemetery was unveiled by HRH the Duke of Gloucester in 2005.

One of the greatest challenges facing the Commission today is that of climate change. Charged with caring for cemeteries and memorials in perpetuity, the horticultural teams in particular have more interest than most

Opposite:
On 5 July 2007 the remains of Private Richard Lancaster were laid to rest in Prowse Point Cemetery in Belgium in the presence of his granddaughter, ninety-three years after he was killed. His remains had been uncovered during construction work near Ypres.

A large part of the work of the Commonwealth War Graves Commission is the care of headstones and memorial panels.

in how their work will be affected in the future. The Commission is aware of the need for responsible environmental management and in many of the countries where it works water is a valuable resource, so that it has to balance its use of water with the needs of the local population and also ensure minimal wastage. For example, in Egypt there is a newly installed irrigation system at Heliopolis War Cemetery which makes efficient use of water captured from the Nile for night-time irrigation to prevent loss of water by evaporation. However, apart from a few locations, the majority of the horticulture in drier locations is allowed to change with the seasons and bare compacted soil is a characteristic of the cemeteries in such places as Africa.

At Heliopolis in Egypt the Commission has installed an irrigation system that takes water from the Nile at night to water the grass and borders.

Away from the Commission's cemeteries and memorials there is a growing awareness of, and interest in, the state of non-CWGC cemeteries. In South Africa a vast programme of refurbishment has taken place. The Army requested the Commission to report on how best to maintain the hundreds of cemeteries in that country. A key recommendation was for concentration of the graves

The headstones in South African cemeteries are unusual in that the reverse side is left uncut and rough, while the face is highly polished.

The Neuve-Chapelle Memorial, designed by Sir Herbert Baker, commemorates over 4,700 soldiers of the Indian Army who fought in France and Belgium in the First World War. When Zehrensdorf Indian Cemetery in Germany was unmaintainable, a plaque to the 210 men buried there was erected at Neuve-Chapelle.

into one hundred sites in order to make future maintenance easier. The Army's casualty branch agreed to the recommendation and asked the Commission to undertake the £500,000 project as they had the infrastructure in the country to carry it out. This was begun in 2004 and lasted for four years.

A mass burial at Tyne Cot Cemetery, Belgium, early 1920s. It was determined that each man should be shown honour and dignity in death.

Every year a number of bodies are exhumed in the course of normal activities, such as road building or excavation, and each time this occurs the same procedure follows: every attempt to identify the casualty is made and if, as sometimes happens even ninety years on, this is successful, the next of

The funeral of one of the 250 men buried in the new CWGC cemetery at Fromelles, February 2010. The soldiers wanted to show honour and respect to their brothers in arms 93 years after their deaths.

kin are informed and invited to the funeral. All remains, identified or not, are buried with full military honours. In 2009 a major operation, the largest of its kind since the Second World War, was undertaken by the Commission. An Australian amateur historian, after years of painstaking research, claimed to have incontrovertible proof of a mass grave at Fromelles in France. This dated back to July 1916 and, when the meticulous archaeological dig was completed, eight pits, dug by the Germans, were revealed. Six contained the human remains of 250 British and Australian soldiers. For the first time in nearly half a century the Commonwealth War Graves Commission constructed a brand new cemetery, which was unveiled in July 2010, just six years less than a century after the Germans buried the men.

A new cemetery for a new century. Designed by the Commission's architect, Barrie Edwards, Fromelles Cemetery owes much to the tradition of the First World War cemeteries and reflects the fact that the men buried here died in 1916.

The extraordinarily bold and forward-looking determination of the Commonwealth War Graves Commission in 1917 to maintain equality regardless of rank, race or creed stands up as well today as it did when it was first expressed by Major General Macready and will go on being relevant well into the future. On reflection, it can be said that the war cemetery had a very short life, less than one hundred years. It was defined by a rising demand for respect for the ordinary soldier, shaped by the shock of the First World War and built by some of the greatest artistic minds of the early twentieth century.

FURTHER READING

Ascoli, David. *A Companion to the British Army.* Harrap, 1983.

Billière, Sir Peter de la. *Supreme Courage: Heroic Stories from 150 Years of the Victoria Cross.* Little, Brown, 2004.

Geppert, Dominik (editor). *The Post-War Challenge 1945–1958: Cultural, Social and Political Change in Western Europe.* German Historical Institute and Oxford University Press, 2003.

Kenyon, Sir Frederic. *War Graves: How the Cemeteries Abroad Will Be Designed.* HMSO, 1918.

Longworth, Philip. *The Unending Vigil: The History of the Commonwealth War Graves Commission.* Leo Cooper, 1967; revised edition 1985; reprinted 2003.

Quinlan, Mark. *Remembrance.* Authors on Line, 2005.

Stamp, Gavin. *Silent Cities: A Memorial Exhibition of the Memorial and Cemetery Architecture of the Great War.* RIBA, 1977.

Summers, Julie. *Remembered: A History of the Commonwealth War Graves Commission.* Merrell, 2007.

Ward, G. Kingsley, and Gibson, Major Edwin. *Courage Remembered.* HMSO, 1995.

Ware, Fabian. *The Immortal Heritage: An Account of the Work and Policy of the Imperial War Graves Commission during Twenty Years 1917–1937.* Cambridge University Press, 1937.

Polygon Wood cemetery outside Ypres in Belgium is a typical irregular battlefield cemetery.

WEBSITES

Commonwealth War Graves Commission (CWGC): www.cwgc.org
You can search here for information about individual servicemen or
women in the Debt of Honour Register but you can also find information
about the cemeteries and memorials as well as a wealth of material about
the Commission's work.

OTHER WEBSITES
(For information about burials pre-1914 or post-1946)
Bermuda National Trust: www.bnt.bm
British Association for Cemeteries in South Asia (BACSA):
    www.BACSA.org.uk
Find A Grave: www.findagrave.com
Imperial War Museum: www.iwm.org.uk
South Africa War Graves Project: www.southafricawargraves.org
Crimean War Roll of Honour:
    www.angelfire.com/mp/memorials/crimrollindz.htm
War Graves Photographic Project: www.twgpp.org

The fifty-six
men buried in
Sequehart British
Cemetery No.1
died on 2, 3 and
8 October 1918,
giving a clue to the
intensity of the
three-days' fighting
by the 5th/6th
Royal Scots and
the 15th Royal
Highland Light
Infantry (32nd
Division).

PLACES TO VISIT

There are 23,000 burial locations in 150 countries worldwide under the care of the Commonwealth War Graves Commission, half of which are in the United Kingdom. Most cemeteries are open all the time but if you are making a special trip it is worth contacting the Commission to double-check. For information about any cemetery, memorial or burial site you would be advised to start with the CWGC's excellent website, which allows you to search by name of casualty or the name of a cemetery.

The following are some of the author's favourites in alphabetical order by country:

BELGIUM
Bedford House Cemetery, Ypres
Brandhoek New Cemetery, Poperinghe
Langemark German War Cemetery, Passchendaele
Lijssenthoek Military Cemetery, Poperinghe
Menin Gate Memorial, Ypres
St Symphorien Military Cemetery, Mons
Tyne Cot Cemetery, Passchendaele

FRANCE
Etaples Military Cemetery, Pas de Calais
Faubourg d'Amiens Cemetery and Arras Memorial, Pas de Calais
Flatiron Copse Cemetery, Mametz
Hunter's Cemetery, Beaumont-Hamel, Somme
Rancourt Military Cemetery, Somme
St Manvieu War Cemetery, Cheux, Normandy
Thiepval Memorial, Somme

INDIA
Delhi Memorial (India Gate), New Delhi
Kirkee War Cemetery
Kohima War Cemetery

ITALY
Cassino War Cemetery
Granezza British Cemetery, Asiago
  Plateau
Moro River Canadian War Cemetery,
  San Donato
Orvieto War Cemetery, Umbria
Sangro River War Cemetery, Torino di
  Sangro

MALTA
Imtarfa Military Cemetery, Mdina
Pieta Military Cemetery, Valetta

THAILAND
Chungkai War Cemetery
Kanchanaburi War Cemetery

TURKEY
Beach Cemetery, Gallipoli
Canterbury Cemetery, Gallipoli
Lone Pine Cemetery, Gallipoli

UNITED KINGDOM
Botley Cemetery, Oxford
Brookwood Military Cemetery, Surrey
Chester (Blacon) Cemetery, Cheshire
Moreton-in-Marsh New Cemetery, Gloucestershire
Portsmouth Naval Memorial, Hampshire
Tower Hill Memorial, London

At Pieta Military
Cemetery in Malta
the earth is
shallow so that
many joint or
collective burials
had to be made
and graves were
cut into the
underlying rock,
with striking
recumbent
markers that
give the cemetery
its distinctive
character.

INDEX

Page numbers in Italic refer to illustrations.